curious about

THERAPY DOGS

BY CARI MEISTER

AMICUS LEARNING

What are you

CHAPTER TWO

Learning to Care
PAGE
10

CHAPTER ONE

Dogs That Share Love
PAGE
4

curious about?

CHAPTER THREE

Helping Hearts
PAGE
16

Stay Curious! Learn More . . .22
Glossary. 24
Index 24

Curious About is published by
Amicus Learning, an imprint of Amicus
P.O. Box 227, Mankato, MN 56002
www.amicuspublishing.us

Copyright © 2026 Amicus.
International copyright reserved in all countries.
No part of this book may be reproduced in any
form without written permission from the publisher.

Editor: Ana Brauer
Series Designer: Kathleen Petelinsek
Book Designer and Photo Researcher: Sara Hood

Library of Congress Cataloging-in-Publication Data
Names: Meister, Cari author
Title: Curious about therapy dogs / by Cari Meister.
Description: Mankato, MN : Amicus Learning, an imprint of
Amicus, [2026] | Series: Curious about working dogs | Includes
bibliographical references and index. | Audience: Ages 6–9
| Audience: Grades 2–3 | Summary: "How do therapy dogs
help people feel better? Learn about these four-legged friends
in this question-and-answer book for elementary-aged readers.
Include infographics, table of contents, books and websites
for further research, and index"— Provided by publisher.
Identifiers: LCCN 2025012825 (print) | LCCN 2025012826
(ebook) | ISBN 9798892008587 library binding | ISBN
9798892009249 paperback | ISBN 9798892009904 ebook
Subjects: LCSH: Psychiatric service dogs—Juvenile literature
Classification: LCC RM931.D63 M45 2026 (print) | LCC RM931.
D63 (ebook) | DDC 615.8/5158—dc23/eng/20250717
LC record available at https://lccn.loc.gov/2025012825
LC ebook record available at https://lccn.loc.gov/2025012826

Photo Credits: Alamy Stock Photo/Adam Bronkhorst, 3, 17,
eriklam, 11 (second from top), Jim Holden, 5, Spencer Grant,
2, 7, ZUMA Press, 6; Freepik/lifeonwhite, 11 (middle);
Getty Images/AleksandarNakic, 11 (second from bottom),
imagenavi, 11 (bottom), kali9, 8–9, Lisa Maree Williams,
2, 14–15, MediaProduction, 11 (top), skynesher, 10, Thing
Nong Nont, 21; Shutterstock/AnnaStills, 13, Monkey
Business Images, cover, 1, 18–19; The Noun Project/
arista septiana dewi, 22, 23, Sara Paukkeri, 22, 23

Every effort has been made to contact copyright holders for
material reproduced in this book. Any omissions will be rectified
in subsequent printings if notice is given to the publisher.

Printed in United States of America

CHAPTER ONE 1

What is a therapy dog?

Therapy dogs are four-legged friends who help people feel better! They visit people in hospitals, schools, and **nursing homes**. These special dogs bring joy and **comfort** to those who need it most.

WHERE DO THERAPY DOGS VISIT?

Libraries

Nursing Homes

Schools

Hospitals

DID YOU KNOW?
Petting a dog for just 10 minutes can make you feel happier!

A therapy dog's job is to bring comfort with cuddles and kindness.

DOGS THAT SHARE LOVE

How are therapy dogs different from service dogs?

DOGS THAT SHARE LOVE

These dogs love visits from people and enjoy lots of pets.

Service dogs help one person all the time. But therapy dogs help many different people. They spend time with anyone who needs a furry friend. Therapy dogs can be pet and hugged by everyone they visit. A therapy dog and its owner are called a team.

DID YOU KNOW?
There are more than 50,000 therapy dog teams in the United States.

Therapy dog teams are **volunteers** who spread joy wherever they go.

DOGS THAT SHARE LOVE

Who do therapy dogs help?

Many libraries invite therapy dogs to help kids practice reading.

These friendly dogs help lots of people. They help kids read in libraries. They comfort people in hospitals. Some visit college students during test time. Others help people feel better after scary things happen.

CHAPTER TWO

Can any dog be a therapy dog?

Pugs make good therapy dogs because they enjoy being around people.

No. The dogs must be at least one year old. They must be **calm** and friendly. The best therapy dogs are patient. They can't be scared of loud noises or new places. They must love meeting people and getting lots of pets!

GOLDEN RETRIEVER

LABRADOR RETRIEVER

POODLE

PUG

BEAGLE

TOP THERAPY DOG BREEDS

How do therapy dogs learn their job?

They take special classes with their owners. They learn to be **gentle** with people of all ages. They practice staying calm around wheelchairs and beeping medical equipment. Therapy dogs must pass a test to show they're ready.

Some therapy dogs visit people's homes to get used to wheelchairs.

LEARNING TO CARE

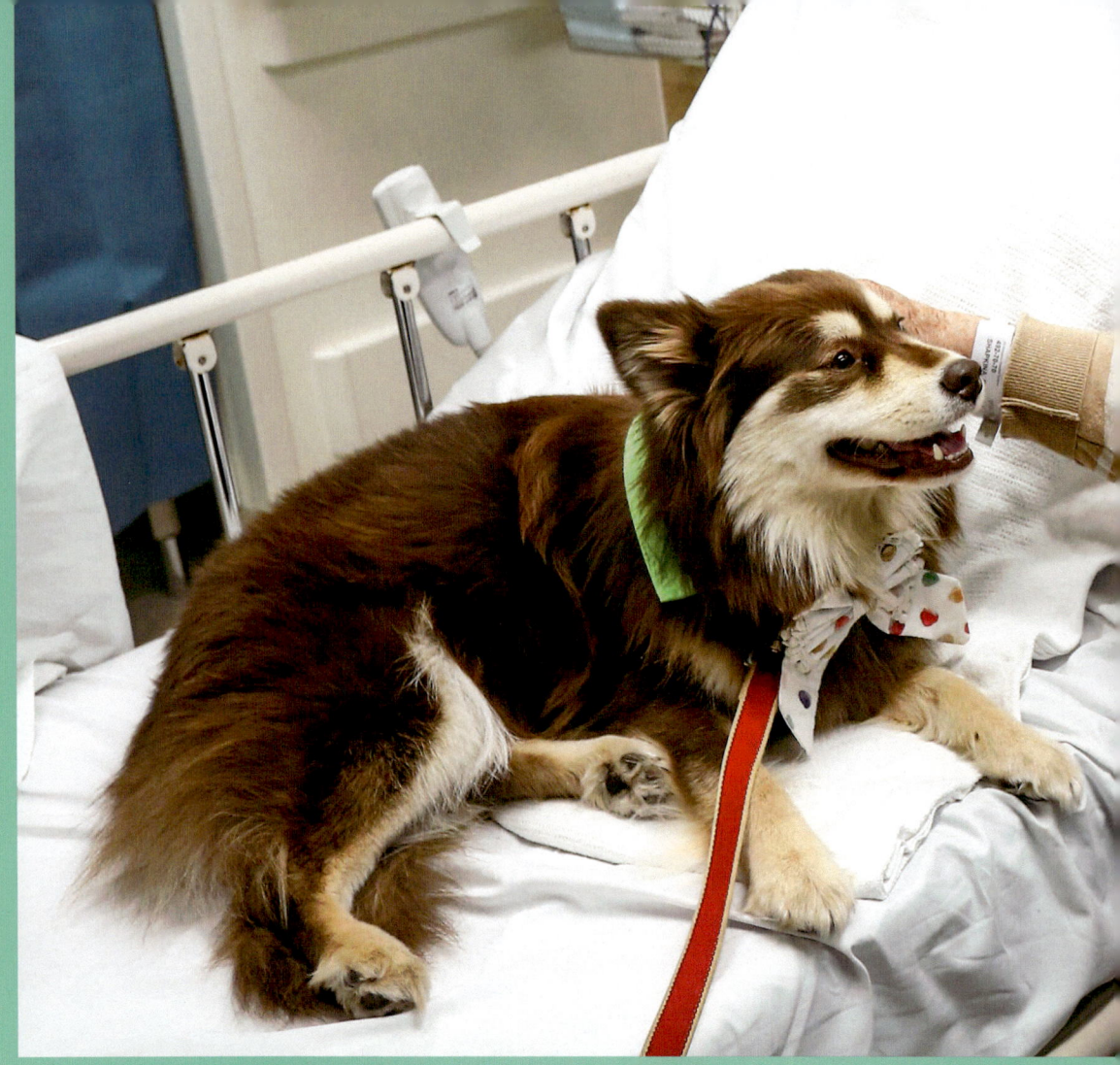

How can I spot a therapy dog?

Therapy dogs visit people in the hospital to make them feel happy and less lonely.

DID YOU KNOW?
Some therapy dogs have their own trading cards to give to people they visit!

Therapy dogs wear special vests or bandanas. These show that they are working dogs. They look happy and calm when meeting new people. Therapy dogs stand still for petting. They don't bark or jump up. You will see many kinds of dogs doing this special job.

CHAPTER THREE

How do therapy dogs help people?

Therapy dogs make people happy! Petting a soft dog helps people feel calm. Throwing a ball to a dog encourages sick people to move more. Reading to a dog makes kids feel brave about reading out loud. They bring joy and a needed **distraction** for people with long hospital stays.

DID YOU KNOW? Some therapy dogs visit more than 100 people each month!

Kids can build reading skills by reading to therapy dogs.

HELPING HEARTS

What do therapy dogs do during visits?

Each visit is different. Some dogs might sit quietly while someone pets them. Other dogs do tricks to make people laugh. Some dogs lay in bed with sick children. Others visit people who are sad after losing a loved one.

A therapy dog can make a sick child feel happier.

Do therapy dogs get tired?

Yes! Helping people feel better is hard work. Therapy dogs take lots of breaks. They only visit for a short time each day. Then, they go home to rest and play.

Therapy dogs take breaks to rest and relax, just like people do.

HELPING HEARTS

STAY CURIOUS!

ASK MORE QUESTIONS

What do therapy dogs do in hospitals?

Can my dog be a therapy dog?

Try a BIG QUESTION: How do animals help humans feel better?

SEARCH FOR ANSWERS

Search the library catalog or the Internet.
A librarian, teacher, or parent can help you.

Using Keywords
Find the looking glass.

Keywords are the most important words in your question.

?

If you want to know about:
- therapy dogs in hospitals, type: HOSPITAL THERAPY DOGS
- your dog being a therapy dog, type: THERAPY DOG TRAINING

LEARN MORE

FIND GOOD SOURCES

Here are some good, safe sources you can use in your research. Your librarian can help you find more.

Books

Therapy Animals
by Julie Murray, 2020.

Therapy Dogs
by Megan Cooley Peterson, 2022.

Internet Sites

Pet Partners
https://petpartners.org
This organization trains therapy animals and explains how they help people.

Therapy Dogs International
https://tdi-dog.org/KidsCorner.aspx
A kid-friendly site about therapy dogs with stories and pictures.

Every effort has been made to ensure that these websites are appropriate for children. However, because of the nature of the Internet, it is impossible to guarantee that these sites will remain active indefinitely or that their contents will not be altered.

SHARE AND TAKE ACTION

Ask your librarian if there's a "Read to a Dog" program at your library.

Make thank you cards for therapy dogs who visit your school or library.

Practice teaching your dog to be gentle and calm like a therapy dog.

GLOSSARY

calm Quiet and peaceful; not upset.

comfort To help someone feel better.

distraction Something that makes you stop thinking about something you don't want to think about.

gentle Soft and kind; not rough.

nursing home A place where people go to live when they need extra care.

volunteer Someone who does something without being forced to do it.

INDEX

breeds, 11
comfort, 4, 5, 9
hospitals, 4, 9, 15, 16
libraries, 4, 9
reading, 9, 16, 17
schools, 4
teams, 7
vests, 15
visits, 4, 6, 7, 9, 13, 15, 17, 18–19, 20

About the Author

Cari Meister has written many books for children about dogs. She recently rescued a Great Dane puppy from an animal shelter. Cari coordinates reading programs with therapy dogs at her local library, where she sees firsthand how these gentle animals help children relax and enjoy books. She lives in Vail, Colorado.